# RADIO TIPS

Mark Lipsky

Design and Layout by Octo Design Group, Inc., Philadelphia, PA
www.octodesign.com

**I love radio.** No other medium touches my life in such a personal and intimate way, despite the fact that thousands of others are tuned to the same stations, enjoying their own one-on-one experience.

In youth, radio provided the soundtrack for my Wonder Years. There are songs forever tied to my first kiss, my first love and my first heartbreak. Today, news and information stations bring me the million-and-one facts I need to stay ahead of the curve.

In college, I interned at WMMR-FM, one of America's great, heritage rock stations. After graduation, I began an amazing 10-year run as Director of Advertising & Promotion at WPEN+WMGK in Philadelphia, including four years on the corporate level for parent company, Greater Media.

For the past 12 years, I've led a remarkable group of people at The Radio Agency, better known as Radio Direct Response, one of America's few "radio only" advertising agencies. From the "agency side" of the business, I've been able to put my knowledge of radio marketing to work for hundreds of clients, both local and national, branders and direct marketers.

This printed collection of Radio Tips represents the best of what I've learned to make radio advertising work.

My thanks to everyone who has touched my life along the way and made it possible for me to enjoy a tremendous career doing what I love.

**Mark Lipsky**     **mark@radiodirect.com**     **amfmradio@aol.com**

# RADIO TIPS

Mark Lipsky

# AND NOW, A WORD FROM YOUR DOG.

Or your cat. Or the late Dr. Milton Connolly. Any of these offbeat introductions would be enough to catch your attention and engage you to listen to what comes next. Startle, shock or surprise with the opening line of your radio commercial and you'll have more listeners paying attention when you get around to asking for the order.

1

# SO, HOW MUCH DID YOU PAY?

Just like seats on an airplane, the next five advertisers on any radio station likely paid five different rates for the same 60 seconds. And while you're unlikely to ever get a "written guarantee" that you're paying the absolute lowest rate, radio sales reps expect to haggle over price. After all, you are bidding on thin air. Everything is negotiable.

# GET HORIZONTAL.

Even though it's "on" 24 hours a day, the typical radio listener doesn't listen around the clock. As creatures of habit, we typically listen to the same stations and programs at roughly the same times every day. To drive your message home, consider buying just one daypart (AM Drive, Midday, PM Drive, Evenings, Overnight) every day. This "horizontal frequency" will cost efficiently deliver your message to your target audience enough times for them to take action.

# (AN YOU HEAR ME NOW?

Got a unique benefit you want consumers to remember? Name it! Or create a catchword or phrase that's fun to say and invites consumers to remember your brand. People with happy feet are "Gellin'" with Dr. Scholl's. Ducks no longer quack. They "AFLAC!" Work your way into everyday speech and boost your brand equity. Can you hear me now? Good!

# WHAT ARE YOUR MEASUREMENTS?

Many direct response marketers leap into radio not knowing what to expect. Develop a game plan. Forecast a targeted cost per lead. Set realistic closing rate goals for your call center. Project your average sale. Then watch those numbers like a hawk and tweak any under performing components of the equation, rather than just shrugging and saying "radio doesn't work." Many of radio's most successful marketers worked their way through disappointing early returns to turn their campaigns into year-round moneymakers.

# SLIDING DAY PARTS.

So what is "Morning Drive?" Ask four stations and you may get four different answers: 6-10 AM, 5-9 AM, 5-10 AM or even 5:30-10 AM. Yet, a commercial aired at 7:58 AM will reach many more listeners than one aired at 5:02 AM. Still, many stations charge the same rate for those two time slots. Pay attention to daypart parameters and spot placements to get the most for your money.

# UNLUCKY SEVEN.

When choosing the best available phone numbers for a Direct Response radio ad, avoid the number seven. Unlike the other digits from one to nine, seven is the only number that contains two syllables. If you're announcing your toll-free number four times, those four mentions of "seven" will add an extra two seconds of copy that would be better spent promoting your brand or selling your offer. Choose "888" numbers over "877" toll free numbers for the same reason.

# STAR POWER.

James Earl Jones for Verizon. Dick Cavett for Courtyard by Marriott. William Shatner for priceline.com. There's nothing like star power to give instant credibility to a product or service, or at least minimize button pushing. For example, priceline.com ran its successful radio campaign to launch and build brand for well over a year before it ever ran a single TV commercial! Recognizable celebrity voices can shorten radio's time line from launch to profitability.

# NO STAR POWER.

If you can't afford to hire Martin Sheen as the celebrity voice of your brand, consider creating a spokesperson. Whether it's an employee of the company (like David Oreck for Oreck Vacuums) or a consumer testimonial ("Hi, I'm Lisa Smith and this week I lost another 3 pounds on the Trim-Now Diet"), having a recognizable voice can jumpstart a brand launch on radio.

9

# ONE LITTLE PHRASE.

**10**

Direct mail marketers know the night-and-day difference changing one word can make. Or a headline. Or the color on the outside of the envelope. The same holds true for radio. So while "50% off" means the same as "Two for One" and "Buy One, Get One Free," you'd be surprised at how a subtle change in copy can change your cost-per-lead. Once you have a profitable "control" spot in place, test these subtle changes on smaller stations, tracking results and changing your control spot when results improve.

# ACTORS VS. ANNOUNCERS.

Use caution and common sense when casting talent for your radio commercials. Many hours have been wasted in recording studios trying to coax golden-throated radio announcers to sound more natural, like "the guy next door." As a rule of thumb, it's generally best to use announcers for announcer copy while hiring actors to play character roles.

# THAT'S WHY THEY CALL IT BACKGROUND MUSIC.

**12**

It's no coincidence that most successful Direct Response campaigns feature no background music, or use brief musical "stings" used only to emphasize copy points. While background music often makes a commercial "sound better," it also permits the listener to divide his attention between your important message and that snappy tune in the background. That's not to say you should never use background music. But don't assume that you're supposed to use it, simply because you can.

# WHAT MAKES YOU LISTEN?

In your everyday life, pay close attention to the things that make you eavesdrop. "I'm going to let you in on a little secret." "Shhhh, don't tell anyone but…." "I never thought I'd say this but…." Take note when a particular phrase grabs your attention. Then see if those words could help you grab a listener's attention in your next radio ad.

# DON'T SELL ME, I WANT TO BUY SOMETHING.

Remember the last time a store clerk asked "Can I help you?" and you automatically said "No" even though you really did need their help? Treat every incoming radio lead as if they've called your phone center to buy something. Don't sell them. Something about your ad motivated them to call. Learn what and why, and then help them buy it. Remember, everyone loves to buy things. But most people hate to be sold.

14

# VERY FUNNY.

Two lizards are sitting on a log. One lizard makes a wisecrack about a ferret. The ferret walks by and jabbers something unintelligible. Thirsty yet? Believe it or not, the radio versions of Budweiser's talking lizard TV ads win radio creative awards year after year. But honestly, do you think they sell a single mug of beer? Why guess? Keep your radio advertising simple. And remember, "asking for the order" means a lot more than saying "Anheuser Busch, St. Louis."

# ONE BENEFIT.

Of the 1,001 reasons a consumer may have to use your product or service, which one is most likely to trigger consumers into action? Ask them! Then present that benefit clearly in your commercial and couple it with a compelling offer and an urgent call to action. In DR radio, this approach yields far greater response than an endless laundry list of benefits intended to appeal to every possible customer.

16

# DON'T PLAY FAVORITES.

Just because WXYZ is your favorite radio station, that doesn't mean it's your best choice to reach your target audience. Even if it does "reach" them, it still may not be a good "direct response" radio station. Trust your DR media agency to steer you in the right direction based on statistical history and keep your favorite radio station as your personal favorite.

17

# GIVE IT A REST.

**18**

You've launched your radio campaign, achieved your target CPO and you can't shovel the cash at radio quick enough. Want to improve your ROI? Give it a rest! Chances are you could flight your campaign and take off every fourth or fifth week. Airing 4 out of 5 weeks, for example, would cut your media costs by 20% but most likely wouldn't cut 20% from your total sales. This tactic could also help you with internal scheduling to manage employee vacation time or days off.

# IN THE WEE SMALL HOURS.

DRTV rings the register in the late night hours, when costs are low and time is available. Third-shift workers and insomniacs are fiercely loyal to radio, whether it's a highway companion like the "Truckin' Bozo" or radio's paranormal talk magnet "Coast to Coast AM." These and other late night radio shows may be worth a test if your inbound phone center operates 24/7.

# CONTROL YOUR TESTING VARIABLES.

Too many first-timers in DR Radio make the mistake of testing too many variables in their commercials. Take, for example, one advertiser who tested two spots: The first ad presented a "hard" offer, while the second served up a "soft" offer. The second ad promised a "free gift" not offered in the first ad. It also featured client testimonials, which were not included in the "straight read" commercial initially aired. With so many variables, the client will never know which change improved or decreased response. Keep it simple. Change one variable at a time and manage your results.

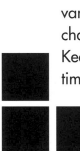

20

# IS YOUR AD AGENCY BEING KEPT IN THE DARK?

So many DR marketers make the fatal flaw of not sharing daily sales and call data with their advertising agency. When the campaign fails, this practice generates more finger pointing than Bill Clinton in a donut shop. Give your ad agency their report card every day. Better yet, enable your agency to access "real time" call and sales data over the Internet. Knowledge is power - and in this case - more efficient media buys and lower lead costs.

**21**

# IS LENGTH REALLY IMPORTANT?

Here are the standards for radio. Local spot radio runs :60. National network and syndicated programs sell in :30 units. News, weather, sports, business and traffic sponsorships offer :10 opportunities. Now here's the scoop. National :30s offer the best buying efficiencies and many DR companies can get results in just 30 seconds. Local :60s give you twice the time, but at a higher CPM than national. As for the :10 sponsorships, by the time you give out a phone number twice, you'll be lucky to squeeze in your company name. Recommendation: Test locally. Roll out nationally.

22

# EVERYONE'S NUMBER ONE.

For some reason, every radio rep seems to claim their radio station is "Number One!" They're trained to scour hundreds of pages of ratings to find their niche. They say, "We're number one!" but they don't tell you that they're Number One with Men 35-54 years of age, between 2 and 3 in the morning. If you choose to deal directly with stations and networks, rather than through a DR agency, ask your sales rep for the contact names and numbers at DR companies who advertise regularly on their stations. Then, check their references just as you would with a new hire.

# RADIO'S WHITE SALE.

**24**

Get ready for the lowest radio advertising rates of the year, come January. Radio stations and networks traditionally experience a significant drop in demand once the holiday retailers fly home with Santa. That opens a window for low rates, from late December through the beginning of February, even though listening levels remain high. Coupled with New Year's Resolutions to self improve, January's low rates make this your best window of opportunity to rush to radio!

# NO, NOTHING'S NOT WRONG.

Avoid the use of double negatives in your advertising copy. Aside from the possible confusion over content, you waste precious syllables to say something in a negative way that could be stated more succinctly in a positive way. Promoting a benefit sells more product than promising the avoidance of a negative.

25

# REPEAT THAT PHONE NUMBER.

If the goal of your ad is to make the phones ring, repeat that number at least three times during your commercial. Anything less is a throwaway. And try different ways of stating the number on everyday people, to see which gets remembered. Is "3652" better stated as "3-6-5-2" or "36-52?" Ask enough people to find out before you record the commercial.

26

# DANGER AFTER DARK.

Ever notice how your AM radio can pick up faraway radio stations after dark? That's due to a phenomenon called "sky waves." To protect certain radio stations on a given frequency (e.g. 950 AM) from outside interference by other stations, the FCC requires some stations to redirect their signal or "go dark" after sunset. So if you're buying airtime on an AM station, make certain that their coverage area doesn't disappear when the sun does.

# WIN AWARDS OR SELL PRODUCT: PICK ONE.

Clever, funny radio commercials rarely move the needle in direct response. In the world of spend-a-dollar-make-back-two, "being creative" takes a distant backseat to the one and only reason you should ever spend a dollar on media - to get results. Don't let your copywriters forget this when crafting your radio copy.

**28**

# MAKING RADIO STATIONS ACCOUNTABLE.

Very few advertisers tell a radio station or network sales rep exactly what they need from the campaign. That leaves the sales rep in a weak position to help you get it. For example, if you know you need a $13.50 cost per lead - and after a test the station delivers a $20.00 cost per lead - you can both reasonably assume that the station would "work" if the ad rates were cut by 35%. A sales rep who can show his sales manager the facts in black-and-white will often times find a way to get you on the air at rates that will make you both winners.

**29**

# LOOK WHO JUST DROPPED IN!

Would your product or service make for an entertaining segment on a radio morning show? Try creating three or four scenarios for a morning show segment that would run anywhere from 5 to 10 minutes. Then, try pitching the event to a radio talk show producer in a small or medium market. If you find your way on the air, work out the kinks in Peoria before you play Chicago. Morning show demonstrations provide great exposure at a great price.

# DON'T RUN TV ADS ON RADIO.

Many TV advertisers make the costly mistake of "lifting" an audio version of their TV commercial to run as their radio commercial. TV copy is written to complement TV's images. In radio, you create images with words, sound effects and musical elements that must stand on their own without the benefit of visual cues. If your words can't paint the picture, your listeners will see an empty canvas.

# EQUAL DISTRIBUTION.

**32**

You just purchased 10 commercials to air in "Morning Drive." The phone doesn't ring. You write off radio as a failure. A month later, you learn that all of your Morning Drive spots aired between 5:30 and 6:30 AM. By law, a station can do that if they define Morning Drive as 5:30-10 AM. But fair business practice and common sense should provide even spot distribution in the 5, 6, 7, 8 and 9 o'clock hours. Ask for spot times before your campaign airs to police the spot placement and maximize your return on investment.

# GOOD WEATHER FOR MARKETING.

America can't wait for winter to end. Why
not let your brand be their guide? Use your
radio ad to suggest five ways to prepare for
spring, featuring your brand in one or more
of the tips. Then, marry your brand to the
nostalgic joys of summer. It's a timely way to
tie your brand to the most eagerly awaited
events of the year - the change of season.

# KEEPIN' IT REAL.

"I lost 200 pounds in four weeks!" Uh huh. Sure you did. Many consumers know that when something sounds too good to be true, it usually is. The best way to keep it real - and protect yourself - is to create a document that must be signed by the client/agency, the radio station and by the person who is making the actual claims. Because while we can't be in all places at all times to verify every claim made during a live commercial, a signed agreement attesting that he/she will only make truthful statements is wise documentation to have should your claims be called into question by a higher power.

34

# WHAT'S THE FREQUENCY?

Don't expect the first-ever airing of your radio commercial to blow out your phone system. Radio is a frequency medium. A typical radio listener needs to hear your message three or four times within a short time frame (a week or two) to actually hear your message, process the information, decide if they need your product or service and then take action. That's not to say your phone won't ring at all on Day One. Just be aware that a first impression of "Who?" will be more common than "Wow!"

# RADIO CALLS VS. TV CALLS.

Since a typical TV viewer is paying full attention to the screen, incoming calls to your phone room will deliver a better-informed lead. That's why it's so important to have intelligent, well-trained sales agents - rather than minimum-wage order takers - handle your leads from radio.

# REINVENTING THE WHEEL.

When faced with the creative challenge of writing radio copy, many direct marketers feel the need to "get creative." Do your bottom line a favor and remember the DR adage to "copy smart." If every commercial you hear for a competitor's product uses a straight announcer read, don't think you need to hire the Vienna Boy's Choir just to be different. If your competitors are still on the air for more than a month, chances are, it's because their advertising is working.

# ONE BAT, ONE BALL.

A one-man company complained about getting too few leads from radio. He aired his commercials on the top-rated stations, but was the only person answering the phone number announced in the ad. He closed three out of 10 leads but claimed he didn't get enough leads. So we offered a baseball analogy and agreed he'd get three hits in his next 10 at bats. Next we asked if, as a batter, he'd want the pitcher to pitch 10 balls at once or one at a time. (Airing on the top-rated stations meant a few, high-priced commercials were generating too many calls at once.) We reallocated his media dollars across smaller stations and spread his phone inquiries throughout the day. Sales soared and another baseball analogy entered the annals of direct marketing.

# UNDERMINING URGENCY.

As tempting as it may be to promote both an "800" number and a Web site URL, one does undermine the other. Let's say you've done an excellent job of grabbing the listener's attention, presenting the unique product benefit, serving up a compelling offer and that you've created a sense of urgency and drilled home the phone number. The minute you mention your Web site in the same commercial, you tell listeners, "It's OK. Don't call now. Check us out on the Web when you get home." You can imagine how many people will forget about you then and there. Radio does an excellent job of driving call volume and Web traffic. But trying to do both in the same spot will often result in you selling less by trying to sell more.

# PERFORMANCE PERKS.

One of the most frustrating parts of a DR radio campaign is generating a terrific cost-per-lead, but failing to close a high enough percentage of sales. Think outside the box for some new incentives that can raise results in your call center. Preferred parking. A week of limousine service to and from work. A night on the town. Cash is king, but sometimes it might take a little creativity to get more from your call center's top performers.

# PICK A DAY AND OWN IT.

Rather than spread out 10 commercials over the course of a week on one station, why not air them all in one day? Target a station with long TSL (time spent listening) patterns and "own" a Monday or Tuesday. Not only will you deliver the needed 3x frequency in a single day, you'll probably enjoy a lower spot rate than retailers who drive up prices with demand for Wednesday-Friday spots to promote weekend shopping. The tactic is called "Vertical Frequency." Consider getting vertical!

41

# "~~HERE'S~~ $1,000. FIND OUT IF RADIO WORKS."

**42**

Under-funded campaigns are perhaps the #1 reason why first-time advertisers walk away grumbling that radio doesn't work. Even though you know your product intimately, the average consumer has probably never heard of you. Allow ample time - at least three weeks - for the radio listener to hear your ad 3, 4, 5 times so that they can "get it," decide if it's right for them and then take action. Otherwise, save your money and enjoy a nice dinner out. You'll probably get the same sales return, but at least you'll have a good meal.

# YOUR GRANDFATHER LOVES RAP MUSIC.

Imagine the traffic-stopping, attention-grabbing impact of a wheezing, 90-year old man hip-hop-rhyming the benefits of your brand. Or a seven-year old calmly espousing the benefits of variable annuities. Sometimes, the silver-tongued announcer or casting-call Soccer Mom isn't your best choice to break through the clutter. Think beyond the usual suspects.

# PIGGYBACK.

McDonald's has been doing it for years. They divvy up a 60-second radio commercial and piggyback a 30-second spot promoting breakfast foods with a 30-second spot promoting their lunchtime menu. The same technique works great for any product or service. Imagine a 30-second testimonial ad, promoting one benefit of your product or service ending with a call to action. Now imagine a different 30-second testimonial - immediately following the first one - promoting another benefit. For double impact in a single spot, PIGGYBACK!

44

# THE PAUSE THAT INSPIRES.

Sometimes, a little thing like a half-second pause can turn ordinary sentences into grabbers. Listen, in your mind, to the difference between a spot that opens with: "I hate mosquitoes" versus "I HATE......mosquitoes." Same wording, but the deliberate delay almost makes you lean in to the radio in anticipation. This subtle change can mean the difference between an attentive listener and one who changes stations.

# AUTO IMPACT.

A recent research survey distributed by the Arbitron Ratings Company shows that 48% of all Americans (aged 12+) said that "while listening to the radio while in a car (they) heard of a sale or special that motivated (them) to visit a certain store Later That Day!" Coupled with the same survey's finding that 75% of drivers and passengers listen to radio "almost all or most of the times in-car", that's an amazing testament to the power of radio to drive sales.

# FREE LUNCH?  FREE CREATIVE?

Be cautious when working with radio stations that offer to write and produce your commercials for free. Your ads could be written by a seasoned copywriter, a sales rep, an intern or the traffic manager. And chances are, their in-house production team will record your ad along with the others they churn out daily. Same voice. Different background music. In a tough advertising world where every dollar counts, it generally pays to hire experts to write and produce, rather than getting "a deal" for free.

# LESS IS LESS.

Some local radio stations have been trying to shift the advertising standard from 60-second to 30-second spots in an effort to cut commercial clutter. That's bad news for DR advertisers who truly need 60 seconds, not 30, to sell their products. Unless your brand is a household name, stick to :60s to get the best return on investment.

48

# I USE IT.  I LOVE IT!

First person testimonials from air personalities can work wonders for direct response advertisers. You'll most likely pay a premium for the airtime and/or a talent fee to the DJ, but the spike in sales can more than cover the cost. Before the first airing, ask your station rep to have the air talent record a sample spot for you to hear. That's one way to make certain that they know what they're talking about and lend credibility, rather than come across as a hired gun who's simply going through the motions.

**49**

# THE DREADED FORMAT CHANGE.

Any time a radio station changes format, the first thing it does is chase away its old listeners who no longer find the new format to their liking. Next comes the task of luring and keeping new listeners. Unless the format change is a subtle one (e.g. Alternative to Modern Rock), you'd be wise to wait for a ratings book to make sure the air time you're buying is more than just air.

50

# SING IT, BABY.

There's nothing like a catchy tune to drive home a message. One regional mattress company sings their phone number. And millions of radio listeners know that "1-800-M-A-T-T-R-E-S" is the number for Dial-A-Mattress. This once-local radio advertiser grew their business on radio by using that catchy jingle to build their brand and drive sales. Should you be asking for the order in the key of E-Minor?

# 2 X 7 OR 7 X 2 ?

If you're looking to "test the waters" on radio, you're better off buying a 7-week schedule in 2 markets, rather than a 2-week schedule in 7 markets. Why? Because your commercial is interrupting the listener's program. They don't care about the commercials. They don't know your brand. It's going to take repeated exposure to your message for the listener to hear it, get it and decide to take action. Like the race between tortoise and hare, in radio advertising, slow and steady wins the race.

52

# WRITING COPY FOR "LIVE READS."

When most agencies entrust air talent to read live commercials, they provide bullet points and hope the talent will choose the right ones to create the strongest sell. Before you provide that list of copy points, know which one is the strongest and instruct the talent to build the commercial around that point. Hammer home the phone number 3-5 times and give clear direction on what must be included in every read. This precaution will minimize rambling and maximize results.

# HOT TICKETS.

Every market hosts a slew of summertime concerts, from Hip-Hop to Soft Rock. Consider buying a small batch of tickets to a series of shows and offering an exclusive promotion to one radio station to give them away. Insist on a 10-second "promotional spot" in every promotional announcement and then negotiate as many plugs as you can for each giveaway. In many cases, you'll get tremendous media exposure (compared to a standard spot buy) and gain the subconscious affinity benefit of partnering your brand with your target's favorite radio station.

**54**

# BUY FALL IN SUMMER.

If you buy an airline ticket in July for Thanksgiving Weekend, you'll probably get a great rate. Wait until November 10th and you'll be paying top dollar. The same holds true on radio. If you know that you're going to be advertising in Fourth Quarter when rates are historically at their highest, place the buy during summer, rather than fall. And give yourself a safety net by negotiating a cancellation clause, just in case.

# MORE WRITERS, MORE CHOICES.

There's an infinite number of ways to script a radio commercial, so why use just one writer? Our agency uses four (sometimes five) writers on every project. This system generates 12-15 creative treatments to evaluate and mix-and-match great copy points. Many times, even the weakest script will contain a great line of copy that makes its way to the final edit. Limit yourself to just one writer and you're, well, limited!

# MORE FREQUENCY, FEWER STATIONS.

The quickest way to drive home your message that magical 3, 4 or 5 times in a week is to beef up your buy on fewer stations, rather than spread across many. After all, a 100 GRP buy could mean that 20% of the population heard your ad 5 times - or that 50% of the population heard it twice. When launching a new brand or product, go with greater frequency, rather than raising the reach.

57

# INTERNET SOURCING.

You've got a great URL, but you're curious to learn which radio stations and personalities deliver the most Internet leads per dollar spent. Here's how. Create a single offer that will play in all your radio ads. Then, create a place on your Web page where listeners can type in the name of the radio station or air talent for a special discount. It's not a 100% pure method of tracking, but it'll let you make some obvious decisions to make your next buy that much more efficient.

# BONUS TIME.

Even though advertising rates drop on nights and weekends commensurate with audience ratings, there's still less demand for those time slots. It's a safe bet that some of the ads you hear on any given night have been given as a "no charge" bonus to loyal advertisers who spend top dollar during prime time. Could you get bonus time for your DR campaign? Ask and ye may receive.

59

# MIDDLE AMERICA IS ON SALE.

Looking for an efficient way to reach "C" and "D" county residents? Try State Networks. In addition to delivering "big fish" radio stations in the major metropolitan areas, State Networks deliver dozens of small market stations in suburban and rural markets. State Networks are an efficient way to buy regionally without having to negotiate dozens of individual media buys.

# THE CHAMELEON.

A little-used, but effective technique in voicing a commercial is when two or more people read the same script and a subtle cross-fade turns one voice into another (e.g. a male voice morphs into a female voice). Often, this lets consumers identify with one of several people offering testimonials, but can also be used, for example, to take a child's voice through adolescence, adulthood and into retirement. It's an ear-catching technique that can greatly improve delivery of your message.

# BUY ME, GET MY SISTER FREE.

In many markets, a handful of companies own most of the top-rated radio stations. It's not often publicized, but if you buy a schedule on (for example) the #2 radio station, you may be able to negotiate a matching schedule on their #15-rated sister station at no extra charge. Just ask!

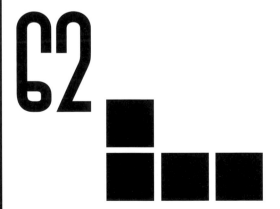

# ENTRY LEVEL NETWORK RADIO.

If you do business throughout America, it makes sense to use the buying efficiencies of network radio, where you'll reach two-to-four times as many people for the same cost of a local market buy. But rather than spend top dollar for top properties (e.g. ABC Prime or Rush Limbaugh), invest $10-30K in a smaller, national network or program to test the waters. Networks like Jones and Salem - and syndicated talkers like George Noory and Michael Reagan - can take an entry-level budget and deliver sufficient numbers to give you a true read.

# SHOW ME THE PRODUCT!

A radio promotion for a major music retailer aired in six of the Top 10 radio markets. To promote the fact that they carried more than just CDs and DVDs, the retailer sent "goodie bags" to the radio DJs, containing Ozzy Osbourne bobblehead dolls, a remote control mini car, a RunDMC action figure and a Kurt Cobain journal. On-air, these goodies added a real "WOW" factor and let the DJs speak firsthand about the great gifts available at the retailer. If you can, send samples to inspire better live reads and testimonials from your air talent.

64

# EARLY WEEK SAVINGS.

Rather than spread an 18-spot radio flight "across the board" on your chosen radio station, why not flight them all to run on two consecutive days? Airing a commercial every hour for nine consecutive hours on both Monday and Tuesday will drive home the message far better than the same 18 spots spread over a five-or-seven-day week. Monday and Tuesday advertisers can also usually negotiate a better rate, as demand for commercial inventory picks up Wednesday through Friday when retailers need airtime to drive weekend traffic.

# LET ME COUNT THE WORDS.

There are few things more comical - and less effective - than an announcer racing through a script with too many words. Many first-time copywriters make the mistake of timing their scripts by running a stopwatch while they read the script silently, rather than reading it aloud at a comfortable, expressive pace. The standard rule-of-thumb for radio copy is 75 words for a 30-second spot and 150 words for a 60-second spot. Toll-free phone numbers count as three words.

# DES MOINES, NOT DENVER.

Many radio campaigns fail because they're under-funded and spend the full budget too quickly. Let your budget size choose your marketplace. For example, you'd be wiser to buy six weeks in Des Moines with the same money that might only buy you two weeks in Denver. Pull the plug too soon and you'll never capture the sale that's only one commercial away from inspiring a consumer to make a purchase.

67

# TEACH ME HOW TO SAY "I LOVE YOU" IN FRENCH.

(Je t'aime.) Or Spanish (Te amo). Or teach me the State Capital of Nevada (Carson City). Find a way to interject an interesting tidbit of knowledge into your radio commercial and you've turned an ordinary sales pitch into something everyday consumers might find interesting. We're all junkies for trivia. Marry your sales message to an interesting fact or conversation starter and your commercial will stand out from the others that simply scream, "Buy me!"

68

# DO IT NOW!

How can you add more urgency to your offer? Is it a "free trial supply" when the customer pays for shipping? Is it a "free gift with purchase?" By definition, all "urgency triggers" center on limitations of time or supply. But, with a cleverly worded urgency trigger ("Get a free month's supply with all of today's orders"), you can imply a limited time offer in a call to action that can run day in and day out.

# RADIO'S LOWEST ADVERTISING RATES.

Broadcast advertising is a supply-and-demand business. In the winter and summer months, demand is low and supply is high. Use that to your advantage by contacting radio stations late each week to scoop up their unsold inventory for the coming week for dimes on the dollar.

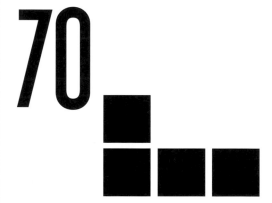

70

# HOW MANY TIMES CAN WE "TAKE YOUR WIFE, PLEASE?"

Using comedy in radio advertising is a risky proposition. In the first place, some listeners won't find the joke funny. And those who do probably won't after they've heard the same joke, week after week after week. If you're going to use comedy, be prepared to freshen the comedy often.

71

# OPPORTUNITIES ON SATELLITE.

While XM and Sirius aren't likely to replace terrestrial radio, they are attracting a slice of the pie that equates to millions of listeners. Their music channels are commercial-free, but their News, Talk and Sports channels do accept paid advertising. Don't overlook the chance to test this medium at a time when rates are affordable.

72

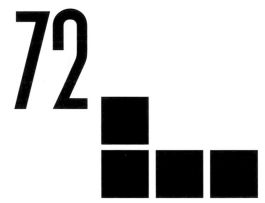

# GET ME OUT OF THIS MESS.

As part of every radio media buy, you should negotiate a cancellation clause in the event that you need to cancel the buy. Do this upfront, as part of your media negotiation. Standard "out" clauses run four weeks for national network and two weeks for local. Naturally, there are exceptions. Some buys are non-cancelable, while others can be nixed with a day's notice. Get your most favorable terms and then get them in writing.

# DEALS AFTER DARK.

Radio's "prime time" is Monday-Friday, 6AM-7PM. That means that advertising rates drop dramatically after 7PM. If your phone room is open until 10PM or 24/7, this allows you to buy some great radio stations and networks, after dark, at a far lower cost than prime time.

74

# DO DIRECT RESPONSE ADS HAVE TO SCREAM TO WORK?

No. They can whisper. They can use dramatic pauses. Or a celebrity spokesperson. Or homespun, friendly voices like Tom Bodett (Motel 6). The key is simply to break through the clutter and be heard. And while many car dealers swear the way to do this is by shouting, finding methods other than yelling will mean less tune-out by listeners who hear enough yelling and screaming in their own homes.

75

# ONE ROCK, MANY PEBBLES.

**76**

20 years ago, an advertiser trying to reach men would simply buy the "Rock" format. Today, there's "Classic Rock" (baby boomers), "Modern Rock" (hard edge), "Alternative Rock" (eclectic new acts), "Adult Album Alternative" (more than just the hits) among others. Rather than just "buying rating points," it's important to understand the subtle nuances in format and the audiences they attract. The primary listenership of the four formats named above run the gamut from 16-year old boys to women in their 50s. Know the difference and you'll see the difference in your ROI.

# PAINTING WITH RADIO.

Compared to visual media, a well-written
radio ad can paint brighter, more vivid
pictures at a much lower production cost.
Verbally guiding the listener to envision the
"perfect sunset" will paint the perfect picture
every time, because it's the "perfect sunset"
in the mind of each individual listener. Try
that in print or television and you'll display
a combination of sky colors and/or palm
tree placement that, by definition, won't be
"perfect" for everyone. Radio is theater of
the mind, with no lighting, wardrobe or
makeup costs.

77

# ONLY ONE WAY TO REACH 'EM.

"Exclusive Cume" is a term used to define those radio listeners who only listen to one radio station. Normally, this occurs because only one radio station in a market carries their type of programming (e.g. Classical Music, Sports Talk, Big Bands, Oldies). Including stations with high exclusive cume is an excellent way to boost your reach in a market place, since exclusive cumers only listen to one station. But even on a test basis, a single station buy on a high exclusive cume station can get quick results, since people who don't share their radio listening with other stations tend to listen longer to that one station.

**78**

# THE 48-SECOND COMMERCIAL.

You've heard it before. You're listening to a nationally syndicated talk show (Rush, Stern, etc.) and a commercial is cut short to rejoin the national network feed after a spot break. This less-than-exact science of local stations cutting into national broadcasts often cuts the tail end of the last commercial played. Was that your commercial? Will you get a make-good? You should. But you may not always get that courtesy. For quality control, get your spot times in advance and monitor the station. If you get cut short, demand a make-good. You might even get "bonus spots" as goodwill from the embarrassed radio station.

**79**

# HELLO, THIS IS ST. PATRICK.

Sometimes, a great attention grabber is a first-person testimonial from a famous historical character. Imagine St. Patrick driving out termites for Terminix. Or Noah speaking on behalf of a basement waterproofing company. Or Hercules for a fitness center. Take care not to infringe on any copyrights, but think outside the conventional casting call for an interesting choice to endorse your products.

# I NEED A NEW REP.

Sometimes, people just don't get along. If you and your radio station/network sales rep aren't seeing eye-to-eye, politely ask for a new one. Don't abuse the privilege, lest you be typecast as the advertiser nobody wants. But if you sense that your rep just doesn't understand your needs and goals, ask the Sales Manager to assign you a new one. Be polite and courteous, but be clear that your goal is to make the change so that you can spend more money on their station/network.

81

# DIFFERENT FORMATS, DIFFERENT VERSIONS.

It's rare that the same, produced radio commercial will sound "right" aired on a Top 40 station, a Country station, a Rap station and a Rock station. For testimonial-driven advertising, the solution is often as simple as using different voices to match different formats. The key is good casting and the foresight of coordinated planning with your media buyers.

82

# WRITE FOR THE EAR, NOT FOR THE PAGE.

By now, you've noticed that these Radio Tips are written conversationally. Casual phrasing. Short sentence bursts. The way people speak. On your way home from work tonight, listen to ten radio commercials and you'll hear at least one spot that was "written for the page," with long-winded sentences that read well on paper, but sound lousy on the radio. Don't fall into the same trap boring public speakers do when they "read a speech." Communicate with people. Don't read at them.

# BUY A PROMOTION.

At certain times of the year, advertising costs soar with high demand. Dance around high rates by using "non traditional revenue" (NTR) dollars to buy the same exposure. A clever concept and a cool prize will often "buy" you a radio promotion that delivers far more exposure than a traditional spot buy. Be aware, though, that you'll need to convey your brand message in a 10-second sponsorship tag, rather than a full 60-second spot.

84

# BAD RADIO CLICHÉS.

Nothing kills good advertising copy quicker than tired clichés. Honestly, does hearing that a retailer has "friendly, courteous salespeople" merit the mention? If so, then make the point rather than "laundry listing" it. "Here at Clothing Retailer, we KNOW clothing - and we'll help you find the right colors and cuts to help you look your best." Aside from killing a radio cliché, this approach transforms a feature into a benefit.

# HOT OFFERS.

There are an infinite number of ways to "ask for the order." Here are some of the latest phrasings tickling the airwaves. Get a 30-day free trial. Get a one-month supply free with any purchase. Get two months of Product "B" free when you order two months of Product "A." Buy Product "A" and get a free gift and keep the free gift even if you return the product. Get a free 30-day trial when you pay shipping and handling. Choose a special twist for your product or service and make it easy for the consumer to say, "Yes!"

86

# DRIVING HOME YOUR MESSAGE.

Overall, "in car" listening accounts for a third of all radio listening at any one time. However, between 5-6PM, over half (51%) of all radio listening takes place inside the car. That's a captive audience glued to your advertising message with little chance of watching TV or reading the newspaper.

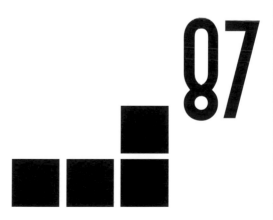

87

# LET'S MAKE A DEAL.

Most radio stations don't like trade (aside from travel and restaurants), but many will entertain a cash/barter deal if there's an abundance of commercial inventory. Plan now for a summer or winter deal that might include something of value the media would want in return for air time. You may need to strike a third party deal, but you may still save 10-50% on your hard costs of advertising.

# PUTTING A FACE ON YOUR BRAND.

Unlike DR advertising that strives to get consumers to "buy now," image advertising on radio creates a mood, a feeling or an attitude about your brand. It might be the friendly, "guy next door" who has a clean hotel room for you (Motel 6) or the paternal, reassuring voice that convinces you that you've chosen the right telephone carrier (Verizon). Paired with radio's ability to surgically pinpoint a niche demographic, branding on radio can be a cost-effective boost to your equity.

# LINE UP YOUR LOCAL ENDORSERS EARLY.

If you're planning a campaign that involves local DJs endorsing your product or service, allow plenty of lead time for them to actually use the product. Your on-air pitch is more likely to be a red hot "WOW" instead of a lukewarm "I'm trying it now."

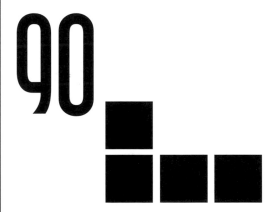

90.

# HOT CARS IN THE SUMMERTIME.

Between Memorial Day and Labor Day, radio stations that traditionally air only "drive time" traffic reports add extra Friday and Sunday coverage as people drive to and from their favorite weekend destinations. A well-placed media buy can drive home your brand with a timely and topical message. ("Stuck in traffic? Wouldn't an ice cold Coke taste great right now?")

**91**

# DAWN DELIVERS.

Perhaps the best-kept secret in radio time buying is the pre-dawn hour from 5-6AM. Most stations still consider this part of the overnight daypart. Others package it as part of Morning Drive. But there are many stations that will let you buy a Monday-Friday schedule, 5-6AM, for just a slight premium above the overnight rates. Check the actual ratings, but in most cases, you'll be achieving a terrific CPM while building frequency by reaching the same audience in the same hour.

92

# SEIZE THE MOMENT.

Many radio advertisers have pre-recorded commercials ready and waiting at radio stations, set to air under the right circumstances. Snow tire manufacturers have standing orders to air campaigns when snow is in the forecast. Power companies have "thank you for your patience" ads ready to roll when storms take down power lines. Is there something unique about your business proposition that, when triggered by a news or natural event, would make it appropriate to have special spots in the can and ready to air?

# HARD-WORKING PHONE NUMBERS.

It's hard to get "great" phone numbers for DR radio. But memorable numbers are crucial for a successful radio campaign. If you're buying local markets, reuse great numbers every 300 miles and have your call center source the calls by incoming area code. For example, 1-800-525-8900 could be used for radio campaigns in Boston, Miami and Dallas and still give you a true read on which radio market generated the call. Avoid reusing numbers in neighboring markets like Chicago and Milwaukee, where a call from Northern Illinois would be impossible to source to one market over the other.

# YOUR PANTS ARE ON FIRE.

There's a big, hairy spider on your shoe. Do I have your attention? Good! A typical radio commercial gives you 3-5 seconds to grab the listener's attention before you "lose" them. Be bold. Be daring. Ask an intriguing question. Challenge their beliefs. Compel them to listen. Otherwise, it's unlikely they'll still be around by the time you ask for the order.

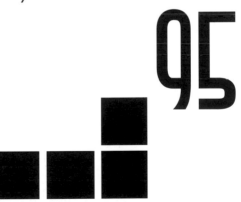

95

# EVERYONE WANTS A REMOTE BROADCAST.

**96**

Except for the radio station. After all, to appease one client and a few hundred listeners attending the remote, they're being asked to compromise their production values by moving the show out of their million dollar studios. Programmers care more about the 30,000 listeners than one advertiser and a couple hundred listeners. One alternative might be to schedule the radio station's "Van Guy" to call in from a location or event, yielding the same net effect for the advertiser. It all starts with a sizeable advertising buy and/or one great idea.

# IS IT "LIVE" OR "LIVE LIVE?"

Be aware that when you pay a premium for a radio station or network personality to voice a commercial, many times you'll be getting a pre-recorded spot, rather than a live read. And while both usually command a premium for the implied endorsement, you should pay less for a recorded talent read than a live read. You get all the value of the talent "endorsement" without paying full price.

**97**

# CREATE A GAME AND OWN IT.

Every once in awhile, a radio contest idea is so good that it becomes an ongoing, 52-week radio feature, rather than a one-or-two-week promotion. Is there a clever twist or angle to your brand that allows for the creation of an "evergreen" radio feature? If so, you can reap year-round benefits from the fruits of a single brainstorming session.

**98**

# LINKING FOR DOLLARS.

Most radio stations have active Web sites with content that changes regularly. With every ad buy - or every promotion - you should be able to create a reason for stations to display your hyperlink logo on their site. Is it a special offer? An online contest? Every incremental sale makes your buy more effective. Plus, you can source every referring link back to its source to measure added value. Some stations charge a fee for this service, while others will award it as added value. Always negotiate.

# 100 GRPs 100 WAYS.

Buying 100 Gross Rating Points (GRPs) means you've bought enough advertising so that everyone in the market, theoretically, would hear your ad once. But since research shows a person needs to hear an ad three, four or five times for it to sink in and generate a response, stagger your media buy so that those same 100 GRPs reach 25% of the population 4x; or 30% of the audience 3.3x. It's all a matter of juggling stations and day parts with the right scheduling software.

**100**

# END YOUR FALL CAMPAIGNS ON DECEMBER 17TH.

Even if you wish to market your products and services between Christmas and New Year's, you'd do well to end your fall campaign before Christmas. Negotiate a new, winter buy to start right after Christmas, during radio's slowest week of the year. You may end up getting that holiday week at half the price - or FREE - as a bonus with your new, winter schedule.

**101**

# LOSSARY OF TERMS AND ABBREVIATIONS

**Average Quarter-Hour (AQH) Persons:** The average number of persons listening to a particular station for at least five minutes during a 15-minute period.

**Average Quarter-Hour (AQH) Rating:** The AQH Persons estimate expressed as a percentage of the population being measured.

$$\frac{\text{AQH Persons}}{\text{Population}} \times 100 = \text{AQH Rating (\%)}$$

**Away-From-Home Listening:** An estimate reported for a listening location outside of the home. It could identify listening taking place either in-car, at-work or some other place.

**Cost Per Gross Rating Point (or "Cost Per Point"):** The cost of acheiving a number of impressions equivalent to one percent of the population in a given geographic group.

$$\frac{\text{Cost of Schedule}}{\text{GRPs}} = \text{Cost Per Gross Rating Point}$$

**Cost Per Thousand (CPM):** The cost of delivering 1,000 Gross Impressions (GIs).

$$\frac{\text{Cost of Schedule}}{\text{Gross Impressions}} \times 1,000 = \text{CPM}$$

*OR*

$$\frac{\text{Spot Cost}}{\text{AQH Persons}} \times 1,000 = \text{CPM}$$

**Cume Persons:** The estimated number of *different* persons who listened to a station for a minimum of five minutes in a quarter-hour within a reported daypart. (Cume estimates may also be referred to as *cumulative* or *unduplicated* estimates.)

**Cume Rating:** The cume persons audience expressed as a percentage of all persons estimates to be in the specified demographic group.

$$\frac{\text{Cume Persons}}{\text{Population}} \times 100 = \text{Cume Rating (\%)}$$

**Daypart:** A part of the day recognized by the industry to identify time periods of radio listening, e.g., Saturday 6AM-10AM or Monday-Friday 7PM-MID.

**Demographics:** This term identifies population groups according to age, sex, ethnicity, etc.

**Exclusive Cume:** The number of different persons listening to only one station during a reported daypart.

**Frequency:** The average number of times a person is exposed to a radio spot schedule.

$$\frac{\text{Gross Impressions}}{\text{Net Reach}} = \text{Frequency}$$

**Gross Impressions (GIs):** The sum of the AQH Persons audience for all spots in a given schedule.

$$\text{AQH Persons} \times \frac{\text{The number of spots in}}{\text{an advertising schedule}} = \text{GIs}$$

**Gross Rating Points (GRPs):** The total number of rating points achieved for a particular spot schedule.

$$\frac{\text{AQH Persons} \times \text{The number of spots in an advertising schedule}}{\text{Population}} = \text{GRPs}$$

*OR*

$$\text{AQH Rating} \times \text{The number of spots in an advertising schedule} = \text{GRPs}$$

**Metro:** Arbitron Metros generally correspond to the Metropolitan Statistical Areas (MSAs, PMSAs, CMSAs) defined by the U.S. Government's Office of Management and Budget. They are subject to exceptions dictated by historical industry usage and other marketing considerations as determined by Arbitron.

**Net Reach:** The number of different persons reached in a given schedule.

**Persons Using Radio (PUR):** The total amount of listening to radio for a particular demo/daypart/geography. The term PUR can refer to Persons or Ratings, AQH or Cume.

**Rating (AQH or Cume):** The AQH or Cume Persons audience expressed as a percentage of the total population.

$$\frac{Persons}{Population} \times 100 = Rating\ (\%)$$

**Share:** The percentage of those listening to radio in the Metro (or DMA) who are listening to a particular radio station.

$$\frac{Station\ AQH\ Persons}{Metro\ AQH\ Persons} \times 100 = Share\ (\%)$$

**Target Demographics:** Audience groups consisting of multiple discrete demographic cells (e.g., Men 18-34, Women 25-54).

**Time Spent Listening (TSL):** An estimate of the amount of time the average listener spent with a station (or total radio) during a particular daypart. This estimate, expressed in hours and minutes, is reported for the Metro only.

$$\frac{\text{Quarter-hours in a time period} \quad \text{AQH Persons}}{\text{Current Persons}} = \text{TSL (in quarter hours)}$$

To express RTSL in hours and minutes:

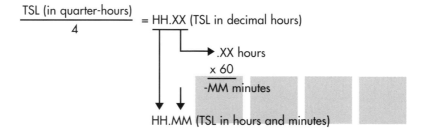

$$\frac{\text{TSL (in quarter-hours)}}{4} = \text{HH.XX (TSL in decimal hours)}$$

.XX hours
× 60
-MM minutes

HH.MM (TSL in hours and minutes)

**Total Survey Area (TSA):** A geographic area that includes the Metro Survey Area and may include additional counties (or counties equivalents).

**Turnover:** The total number of different groups of persons that make up a station's audience.

$$\frac{\text{Cume Persons}}{\text{AQH Persons}} = \text{Turnover}$$

*OR*

$$\text{AQH Rating} \times \frac{\text{The number of spots in}}{\text{an advertising schedule}} = \text{GRPs}$$

**Universe:** The estimated population for an age/sex group in a geographic area.

# NOTES

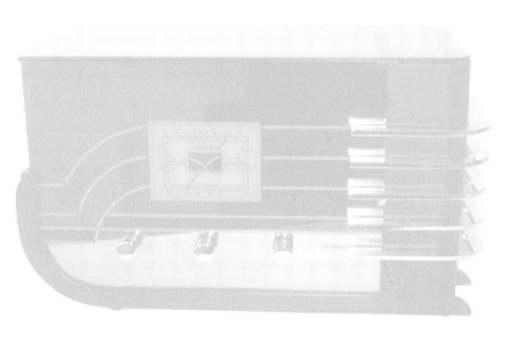

# NOTES

# NOTES

# NOTES

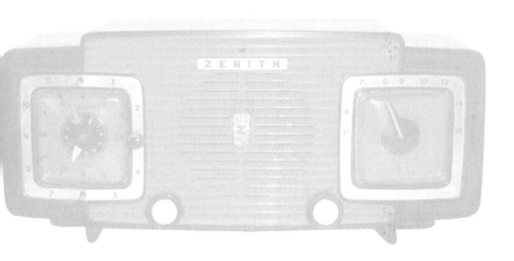